Wherever This All Ends

Wherever This All Ends

Poems by

Leland Seese

Cover art by "Home Fields" by John Singer Sargeant

Cover design by Shay Culligan

ISBN: 978-1-950462-87-2

Kelsay Books Inc.

kelsaybooks.com

**502 S 1040 E, A119
American Fork, Utah 84003**

Acknowledgments

Thanks to the editors of the following publications in which these poems originally appeared:

82 Review: "He Hears My Children's Sermon Differently"

The Christian Century: "As I Fall"

The East Bay Review: "doxology from a barroom window"

Eyedrum Periodically: "Broken"

Ginosko Literary Journal: "Driving My Adult Son to the King Street Station", "Hound of Heaven", "Easter Sunday Evening"

The MacGuffin: "Moving Day"

Sequestrum: "The Fourth Madness", "Merely Human", and "Time Travel"

Sport Literate: "Long Arc" (as "National Pastime"), "Grown Men Playing Catch"

The Stonecoast Review: "The Return of Skinny Ties"

The South Carolina Review: "Dress Shoes"

Third Wednesday: "Torch Song"

The Timberline Review: "The Call"

I would like to thank Kate Lucas, my instructor and editor—without your wise guidance and encouragement this chapbook would not have come into being.

Thanks to my teachers at Hugo House in Seattle—
Elizabeth Austen and David Wagoner.

Thank you to my writer friends for all the camaraderie, critique, and joy—Michele Bombardier, Linda Katz, Michael Jacobs, Shankar Narayan, Ken Wagner, and Lillo Way.

This chapbook is dedicated to my first, best, and most demanding editor, my wife, Lisa. Thank you for never giving up on my mad dream of being a poet!

Leland Seese
Seattle, 2020

Contents

I.

Long Arc

We stretched out on our backs, burning
through our sixteenth summer under fly-ball skies,

twitching sweaty skin on itching grass,
raising mitts as shields against the sun.

Teammates, coaches—all gone home.
Batting practice, shagging flies, done for another day.

Silence, sky. Then Eric said, *Wherever this all ends
it still don't end.*

Beyond the left field fence, brick and terra cotta, classrooms.
Mr. Orr taught calculus, how to track a ball

using differentials, arcing integrals across
a blackboard sky, to prove what fielders know by feel.

I've long-forgotten high school math. Eric lives in Pittsburgh
with five kids, last I heard. *It still don't end—*

out of a long arc, a pearl. A pop, a sting,
the universe in the pocket of your mitt.

Driving My Adult Son to King Street Station

Along the way he points toward a storefront,
Little Saigon. *Dad, pull over there.*
He wants to buy two banh mis from the deli
for his train ride home to California.

Tiny shop, unfamiliar spices, unknown cuts of meat.
Two young clerks are screaming at each other,
curses I am guessing, Vietnamese. Red-faced,
anger cabling their neck veins, until one turns to us,

smiles at my son, says, *Hey, Bro,*
always good to see you back in town!
From icy bed, a long-finned orange fish
smiles up at me,

dead translucent eye that's seen the bottom
of the ocean regards a graying man
whose son—this boy right here!—
will soon be turning 30. I want to tell it

to this fish, the way my belly's full
of coffee, toast, and eggs but I feel hungry.
O sequin-scaled sage, he couldn't stay
my soft-cheeked lad a little longer?

The fish maintains its smile,
blank-eyed, silent gaze. If there's a way
to feed this hunger it isn't in this store
or at the bottom of the ocean.

Dress Shoes

Winchell's donuts after church
depending on Dad's mood.

He could kill an opportunity,
baritone a groaning door
slammed closed,

It'll be a mob scene.

I forgot to shine my dress shoes (once again).
That's the real reason we don't stop.

Ratty chamois, almost empty can of polish
from his own collection,
bad for you to smell, but who could not?

It'll be a mob scene
cancelled Santa's lap down at the Bon Marche,
and the only chance to see the Pilots face the Tigers,
Mickey Lolich pitching for Detroit.

Dress shoes are an agony of toe crunch,
heels bit to bleeding.

Before my brother went to Canada instead of Vietnam,
he tossed my dress shoes in the lake
to spare me from the chore of being ring-bearer
in Dad's wedding to my babysitter neighbor.

As my mom to-be she took me out
to buy a brand-new stupid pair.

Through the reception at the VFW
I snuck champagne. Forced to dance with her,
I bent over and threw up on them.

Merely Human

My next-door neighbor, sometime prostitute
who looks to me to help her
in the art of managing her adolescent son.

We never talk about our work
when we talk across the fence.

I wonder what they make of it,
the passersby who see a Marilyn Monroe
in short-shorts, chatting up a graying gentleman,

or neighbors who remember, *He's a pastor,*
isn't he?

Beneath my collar and my robes,
behind the honorific, Reverend,
I live a merely human life, drinking beer

out in the bleachers at the ballpark,
keeping resolutely seated

beside my Deadhead veteran friend-confessor
who survived the Mekong Delta,
as younger soldiers sing The Star Spangled Banner.

The Fourth Madness, July 4th, 1970

In this world I lock out all my worries and my fears.
—The Beach Boys, "In My Room"

... but they do not understand their condition,
because they do not clearly perceive.
—Plato, "Phaedrus"

Fourth madness strikes.
Teenage boy in bed,

tucked between himself and someone
else's definition. Early morning in his room,

somnambulant along the pathways
of his unexamined life.

Posters on the walls of ballplayers,
the Beach Boys, Raquel Welch.

Does he realize his wings are clipped?
Having been to unseen places in his dreams,

he's plummeted into the underworld,
alarm clock morning, eggs and pancakes,

parade on Main at noon,
beer and Roman candles

after dark. The new girl,
maybe sex.

But in his room, he turns,
hears someone else's definition,

The life you're living isn't
who you have to be.

20

Hound of Heaven

I am the future pastor of your local congregation,
lighting up the day's first Lucky Strike,
sitting in this Perkins parking lot in Minot, North Dakota.

It makes sense now, better than the seminary taught us,
why Jonah in the Bible ran away.

Piloting my Honda 1300, I drifted into town upon a sea
of sunflower fields, August dawn adjusting heaven's light,
delft to white to banking embers on the east horizon.

Let's begin with this: God's preoccupation with the sinner
has forever been mismanaged and misunderstood.

My purple t-shirt is a souvenir from one last night
in New York City. Blood-red dripping letters cross
my chest Vampire Lesbians of Sodom.

I'll bet the Minot Christian population regards
the Vampire Lesbians of New York City as bound

for hell,
even if they're only on a stage in Greenwich Village.
Things didn't go so well for Jonah when he ran away.

So who am I to judge the citizens of Minot,
if Minot is where I'm called to be?

Isn't it the loveliest of mornings? asks the waitress,
smiling, pouring coffee in my cup as I peruse
the Perkins breakfast menu.

Young Couple on a Triumph 750 Motorcycle

Their faces an ecstatic flash
of laughter flying past me

as they cross the empty
Montlake Bridge at five

this warm June morning,
pink and orange folds

of dawn.
Cutoffs, t-shirts, afros,

and she's tucked right up
against his back.

Eyes electrified, arms wrapped
around his waist, she's

burrowing her chin
into his shoulder

as he opens up
the throttle at the spot

where you and I first kissed
when we were young,

stars dissolving into day
the way they do.

Time Travel

You call me all the way from Dingle,
worried I will never understand
the miracle of beehive huts
monks made by hand from
dry-stacked stones 14 centuries ago.

Inside, you say, the light glows
dimly, as if captured on the day
the first monk bent to prayer
beneath the tiny window,
benediction still and swift at once,
fleeting foretaste of eternity.

Your single sob travels from a pub
in County Kerry, to reach me in Seattle,
spanning the Atlantic and eight hours
and a continent.

I want to hold you, make oblation
for your tears. You say it's always
been the same for fools and saints
who try to stay what vanishes
upon arrival, tearing palms and fingertips
on stone.

Broken

We break
things—
ourselves,
each other.
No choosing
harmlessness
from actions
we undertake
or fail to take.

A muffled rumple.
We run over
living things
we see and do not
see
until, too late,
excuses spent,
we break.

Torch Song

Look at him! Just look
at what the years have done.

The hostess leads me through the dining room
        toward him. I refuse

to see myself
an hour ago
before the hotel bathroom mirror. Fluorescent light.
Cringing at the sight of me—
        gray strands threading through
        what once was chestnut hair, liver spots
        on backs of hands, belly lipping over
        waistband. Eczema!—that little island
        of decay between my brows. O Death,
        you stake a foothold on my flesh.

But look at him. Just look!
He can barely reach the table for his girth
as he levers scrambled eggs from plate to mouth.

Seated now before him, I will make my point.
I order coffee.
        Black.

Forty years. The dorms. A floor apart,
reclining on his roommate's bed,
        smoking pot,
        plotting revolution,
        laughing at the National Lampoon.

Toward the end of freshman year he fell in love
and I was out. Sitting with his roommate
on the hallway floor, those noisy thumps inside,
the laughter and the moans,
      with her.

He friended me on Facebook several months ago.
Thrilled to see my post about a conference in Houston—
Hey! I live there! Let me take you out for breakfast,
he had written, at the hotel's restaurant.

They married after college. I had transferred
to another school.

Three kids. *We're blessed,* he says
as he pushes one last strip of bacon in his mouth.

We try rehashing skits from SNL—Belushi, Ackroyd,
alas! poor Gilda Radner—until a silence, then a longer
silence stretches out between us,
heavy as the sweet roll he devours in three bites.

It's so good to see you—now he shakes
his head, and…tears!
*It's a shame we never got together
sooner. Sure you don't have time to come
to dinner at our place?*

Yes. I know I'm sure. Where's the waiter? Where's the need
to try to challenge as he offers, *Let me get the check.*

doxology from a barroom window

the fire engine blasts its horn and siren
southbound toward an elsewhere accident

two women in their twenties drinking vodka
flit about the edges of their readiness to kiss

a cough drop wrapper gold and black
blows up from the gutter to the sidewalk near a tree

a zillion other things in endless rearrangement
these three arranged like this are all i see

II.

Starting Over

Let go from Class-A Lansing, Midwest Baseball League,
    I drive all night along the lesser stretches of the interstate.
A dozen different towns, three exits each, all look the same.
    First, Denny's, mini-mart, and off-brand gas. Black-clad
teens around the pumps, Nirvana t-shirts, cigarettes and cans of
    Monster, inside jokes and dagger-eyes for all outsiders.
Second off-ramp—Main Street, city hall, a tavern,
    hardware store, a war memorial.
Off the last ramp bulldozers are helping realtors to sell a vision,
    former bottomlands as someday neighborhoods with names
like Mountain Valley View Estates, now nothing
    more than unpaved cul-de-sacs and survey stakes.

I pull off at a second ramp in North Dakota, for a nap,
    rising sun lighting up a morning hotter than the stovetop
burning bacon at the Denny's one stop back.
    Seven hours on, the county clerk, his workday folded in his
desk by two o'clock, says to me, young stranger
    in the darkened bar, *Hottest goddam day I can recall*
and I have lived here all my life.
    The TV in the corner broadcasts basement-dwelling
baseball teams from distant coasts, running out their grounders
    even though it counts for nothing toward the pennant.

Buffered by two pints, but still within the legal .08,
    I'm ready for another hundred miles
west across the sweltered continent to drown in the Pacific
    once again the buzz-saw drone of unmet hopes,
passed down from shivered ghosts in Douglas fir limbs
    of Olympic old-growth forests. My grandfather,
the finest topper in the logging camps, long gone.

I'm heading back out to the coast
of Washington, in answer to my widowed mother's prayer,
        to retire mitt and spikes in the old cedar chest,
try to see what might come next.

As I Fall

*...this deep dread...is a great gift from God, for it is the
precise point of our encounter with his fullness.*
—Thomas Merton, "Contemplative Prayer"

The old slough appears in this dream,
mudded, shallow, leeches gathered
in the overhanging grass along the banks.

The barricaded overpass floats forty feet
above the water, closed to buses, cars, and trucks.

It seems the briefest fall to an observer
on the shore. But new awareness comes
when the plunge protracts, weighted
like the purple-orange air of the Grand Canyon,
dusk murmured up its eastern wall.

As I fall, time dissolves into something different
from eternity. I surrender to the dread
and to the peace of being and oblivion.

Death is merely incidental in this dream.
I watch my body as I feel bones crunch
against the earth, and hear my breath pass out of me
by a sort of mystical ventriloquy.

Sprawled on spongy ground beside the overhanging grass
as some vast something brushes past, dangerous
and gentle, I wait with patience to be devoured
or to be given second birth.

The Call

The Word of the Lord was rare in those days;
visions were not widespread.
                                        —I Samuel 3:1

What if something simple as a word
    is not made rare by being seldom spoken? What if
surfeit of relentless senseless verbiage hides the Word
    the way a plague of locusts overwhelms
the light of day? The way a plague of locusts
    over-blows into a single note
to drown all music, wave-invasion over watercourse and wadi
    leaving chalk-dry tongue and palate,
intellect and affect nothing more than desert waste?
    Sound wave, ink and paper,
pixels and electron beams projected on a screen,
    suffusing every room in which
we sleep and wake and copulate and defecate and try
    to gain a paradisiacal oasis as along the way
we all inexorably die.
    Who might find the thing she calls her life
becoming interrupted? Who might hear a new voice,
    brooding and baptismal,
calling, speaking into is-not, *Is,* speaking into void
    and darkness, *Light*? Who might
hear his name the way that Samuel was summoned
    out of dream and into vision,
out of childhood to surpass the priest
    whose voice was busy being garbled
during days in which the Word
    was rare.

He Hears My Children's Sermon Differently

The new boy can't sit still,
hair unkempt and beautiful

as a field of sunflowers. Yellow petals
flare and blind towering Goliath

in his mind.
Words refuse to fall in line.

He shrieks, and someone hisses *Shush!,*
which makes me want to weep.

Boxing his own ears, he slings
a hymnal toward the congregation.

From the choir loft a baritone
calls *Settle down! You'll hurt someone.*

His mother rushes forward,
says *He loves this story,* says,

*He wants to change his name
to David.*

Half a dozen kindergarteners,
narrow shoulders insufficient

for anything but wonderheaded
buzzing, form a gathered hive.

They call him David right away.

The Return of Skinny Ties

A man whom I'd describe as florid
in complexion, character, and lexicon
assessed the color of the knit one as
he helped himself into the seat across
from me one morning at the Café Reggio.
He called it *Aubergine*.
I was 22 and lived in the East Village,
convinced a shitty job in food service
and the squalor that surrounded 8BC
would render me The American Rimbaud.
He must have been around age 60
(my age now), an unclaimed property
badly needing renovation if not outright
demolition.

The leather one, black as cool,
should cool come back in style,
will need some renovation of its own
to mend a cigarette burn branded onto it
at the Palladium at just about the hour
robins launch dawn choruses in May.
War stories. Nothing happened,
really. An actress, a face I recognized
from my sister's *Cosmopolitans*
back home in Sterling Heights, used a Dunhill's
glowing tip to answer *Not a chance*
when I asked her for a dance.
Two weeks later I split up with NYC.

But my collection's *ne plus ultra* is a genuine
Lloyd Johnson just like Madness, just like
"Down by Law". I found it on a visit
to the East Bay in the days of third wave
ska. Rancid and reconstituted Specials.

I cinched it up the other day and took
a table in Seattle where a kid about the age
of one of mine was guzzling cappuccinos
(three empty cups in front of him)
and scribbling in a Moleskin
faster than John Dillinger bled out.
His eyes were saying something halfway
between irritation and indulgence
as I pointed to his sweater with an
observation (in case he didn't know),

That's aubergine.

doxology from an early autumn stroll

daytime moon waning
crescent hammock

take a nap on it
two crows goad

indifferent osprey
across the blue duvet

dandelion seed
caught in diamond

crotch of cyclone fence
desperate corner

of the strip mall
parking lot

tarty autumn
golds and reds

moldy stems
of sunflowers

heads defaced
by hunger-frenzied squirrels

III.

After Grandpa's Stroke, 1965

Grandpa's fastened in his La Z Boy,
a diesel donkey engine bolted to its frame.
Next to him, a plastic bowl, fake cloisonné,
ribbon candy mix sticks together
like a psychedelic school of fish.
Each little fish bound to its brethren
till he wrenches one away, salves
his ash-dry throat, smoking's aftermath.
Cigar breath and Vitalis as I reach
to pat him on the shoulder (he can't
shake hands), aroma of anointing
for his slow and self-inflicted death.

When I was 12, we two stood eye-to-eye.
I'm taller at 18, but still no match in biceps
or in chest, his solid as the cedar trunks
he used to saw in forests south of Forks.
I'm now the age of him and Grandma,
framed in black-and-white beside his bed.
Their wedding day in 1922, her hand
a Douglas fir sprig, resting delicate on his.
Callouses and power in those hands,
those fists, from gripping two-man saws
and axe handles, logging land his father's
generation wrested from the Quillayute,
through treaties they committed to,
but didn't understand.

Now he tires trying to untangle words
jammed tight as logs above the rapids
on the Bogacheil. His aide comes in,
cheerful, though I see her see the storm
clouds bank up in his eyes.

Lunch or nap? her question left to drift
on currents silent as the Hoh where it pours
out wide with undertow east of Oil City.

Mom and I are silent driving home,
currents of her own flow in the rills
and backwaters of pride and suffering.
She parks in our garage and turns to me.
Grandma used to have to drag him
from the bar down on Rainier before
his paycheck disappeared.
She wants me to know why,
when I told him there were jobs in Chehalis
for choke-setters, he unjammed his jaw
and shouted, *Don't!*

Moving Day

These roses, purple long ago, have turned
burnt umber from fifty years of sunlight

blazing through the windows in the entryway
beside the coat rack and oval rug,

printed on the settee's cushion, bright
in memory, now approaching brown,

the only roses Mother never tended.
Her life lived out-of-doors among living things:

children, chickens, apples, dahlias, corn.

Today the movers haul away the harvest
of her years. She will relocate to town,

uprooted, assisted, no longer living
in the rhythm owned by those who sow and reap.

Her protests and refusals long-exhausted,
she perches on the ottoman, a silenced wren

until some wonderment brambles
through her mind, makes her merry.

Picking her words carefully as berries, she calls
attention to the roses spilled across the porch,

purple, bright as half a century of sunlight,
when the young men tilt the settee out the door.

Sudoku

I am craving logic.
Some people have a cigarette
at times like this. I'm chain-

solving sequences of numbers, a detective
in a mystery. You weren't murdered, Mom;
you died peacefully, long-lived.

But still I struggle with a puzzle: we traded
places. I became the parent, you
the child.

I made your medical appointments,
paid your bills, bought your favorite
flavored water (grape).

Toward the end I even fed you
popsicles, holding them the way you held
my bottle in the cow's milk mornings,

bathrobe, curlers, cigarette.
Now I grow inordinately angry
when an 8 could go

in either top or bottom box. And, look!
I've put an extra 2
where one is printed at the other end.

I want to think it isn't me.
It's a faulty puzzle, an act of cruelty
perpetrated by a stranger indifferent to my

grief. And grief it seems to be
that drags me into lightless morning,
where commuter traffic murmurs,

a processional of mourners
on the boulevard. I risk December's sting,
in terrycloth pajamas, barefoot,

surrendered to the temperature
that frosts my breath,
bend down, lift the paper.

Back inside, I shed the layers—
op-eds, sports, the weather, classifieds.
I am focused only on Sudoku's

soothing sense of purpose,
the distraction it provides,
even only for an hour. Even if

what's left to show for all the effort
is a fleeting burst of serotonin before
I undertake the weight of yet another day.

Easter Sunday Evening

Hand in bony hand
we sat silently,
dusk leaching pink
from cherry blossoms,
trees planted down the lakeshore
when our grandparents were young.

You rummaged memory,
trying to go back
to where you'd left your glasses.
I was waiting to find out
what kind of animal—turtle,
muskrat, mud hen—
was making ripples in the water
near an alder felled by windstorms
last November.

You broke a brittle twig
from one of the old cherries,
blackened as a candle wick,
too spent even to host lichen.

How much longer will these trees be here?
you asked, not me. My answer was
to squeeze your hand.

A Return

Warm Midwest mornings
building to June thunderstorms,
our month-old son would lie slack-jawed
along the tenderness of my wife's arms.

Syrup mixed from breast milk
and saliva sliding from the corner
of his mouth, eyelids languid
as the outdoor air, half-mast. I imagined

him communing with eternal love,
origin of everything. My wife, shielding
her reverie, would smile up at me.
He's titty-drunk!

Lightning, here and gone.
But we are never left abandoned
to our days. A gentleness arises
like a distant thunder, like a lullaby,

as I sit slack-jawed at my desk
this heavy-lidded August afternoon,
cloud shadow lowering
along the tender arms of maple trees.

Grown Men Playing Catch

Onto the diamond we bear ourselves
in bone and memory, sciatic,
hypertensive, age gaining
as we venerate our legends,
catch and throw.

Positioned in a square, we grow
as rhythmic as a group of monks
settled to their breath.
We toss the ball in looping arcs,
recite our fathers' almost tenderness,
who tucked their strength inside
the sweatbands of their caps,
their absence now
in death, their absences in life,
who gave us guidance
in the proper grip of seams, the pose
of arm, the art of leaving
all emotion unexpressed,
till after follow through, till snap
of wrist and pop of ball in mitt.

This glove still has some life in it,
one says to lighten up the mood.
Then, *Sorry!* as he skips an errant throw
across the rocks and tufts
wide of his mate, who lifts
the litany, recitative, *That's OK
now; shake it off,* and turning,
spots the ball and gives it chase.

We listen in an attitude of grace,
letting each one in his turn
lengthen little league home runs
or recollect a double play
from forty years ago.
With wistful lies we all confess
a whisper in the infield dust,
a reckoning, as dreams
of being Satchel or DiMaggio
fly past our outstretched gloves.

To the diamond once again, our love
for one another and this game
aching in our ebbing lives, our hearts
still beating out the cadence,
catch and throw.

About the Author

Leland Seese is a Pushcart Prize-nominated poet whose work has appeared in a wide variety of print and online journals. An ordained Presbyterian minister, he has served congregations in Plymouth, Michigan, and Seattle, Washington, where he and his family now live.

CPSIA information can be obtained
at www.ICGtesting.com
Printed in the USA
LVHW051817100620
657784LV00006BA/726